The
THREE
SILLIES

The
THREE SILLIES

Retold and illustrated by

Kathryn Hewitt

Harcourt Brace Jovanovich, Publishers

San Diego   New York   London

To David

Copyright © 1986 by Kathryn Hewitt

Library of Congress Cataloging-in-Publication Data

Hewitt, Kathryn.
　　The three sillies.
　　Summary: A young man believes his sweetheart and her family
are the silliest people in the world until he meets three others who
are even sillier.
　　[1. Folklore—England] I. Title.
PZ8.1.H48Th 1986　　398.2'2'0942　[E]　　85-16375
ISBN 0-15-286855-0

Printed in the United States of America
First edition

A B C D E

The paintings in this book were prepared in watercolor and gouache
　　on 90 lb. D'Arches hot-press paper.
The text type was set in Adroit Light by Thompson Type, San Diego,
　　California.
The display type was set in Floreal Haas by Thompson Type,
　　San Diego, California.
Color separations were made by Heinz Weber, Inc., Los Angeles,
　　California.
Printed by Rae Publishing Co., Inc., Cedar Grove, New Jersey.
Bound by A. Horowitz & Sons, Fairfield, New Jersey.
Production supervision by Warren Wallerstein.
Designed by Dalia Hartman.

Once upon a time there were a farmer and his wife who had one daughter, and she was courted by a young man. Every day he would come to see her and would have supper at the farmhouse. The daughter would go down to the cellar to draw the cider for supper.

One evening she had gone to draw the cider, and she
happened to look up at the ceiling, where she saw an ax
stuck in one of the beams. It must have been there a long
time, but somehow or other she had never noticed it before,
and she began to think.

She thought it was very dangerous to have that ax there, and she said to herself, "Suppose my sweetheart and I were to be married, and we had a son, and he grew up and came down to the cellar to draw the cider, and the ax were to fall on his head—what a dreadful thing it would be!"

She sat down and began to cry.

Upstairs, they began to wonder why she was so long drawing the cider, so her mother went to look for her and found her sitting in the cellar. The cider was running all over the floor.

"Why, whatever is the matter?" asked her mother.

"Oh, Mother!" said she. "Look at that horrid ax! Suppose my sweetheart and I were to be married, and we had a son, and he grew up and came down to the cellar to draw the cider, and the ax were to fall on his head—what a dreadful thing it would be!"

"Dear, dear! What a dreadful thing it would be!" said the mother, and she sat down by her daughter and started crying, too.

After a bit, the father began to wonder what was keeping them so long, so he went to the cellar to look for them himself. There sat his wife and his daughter crying. The cider was running all over the floor.

"Whatever is the matter?" he asked.

"Why," said the mother, "look at that horrid ax! Just suppose our daughter and her sweetheart were to be married and have a son, and he grew up and came down to the cellar to draw the cider, and the ax were to fall on his head—what a dreadful thing it would be!"

"Dear, dear, dear! So it would!" said the father, and he sat down beside them and started crying.

Now, the young man got tired of waiting up in the kitchen by himself, and at last he went down to the cellar, too. There sat his sweetheart and her parents crying, side by side. The cider was running all over the floor. He marched over and turned off the tap.

Then he said, "Whatever are the three of you doing, sitting here crying and letting the cider run all over the floor?"

"Oh," said the father, "look at that horrid ax! Suppose you and our daughter were to be married and have a son, and he grew up and came down to the cellar to draw the cider, and the ax were to fall on his head—what a dreadful thing it would be!"

And then the three of them started crying worse than before.

But the young man burst out laughing. He reached up and pulled out the ax.

Then he said, "I've traveled many miles, and I've never before met three such big sillies as you three. Now I shall start out on my travels again. When I can find three bigger sillies than you three, I'll come back and marry your daughter."

He wished them good-bye and started on his journey, leaving them all crying because the daughter had lost her sweetheart.

The young man traveled a long way.

At last he came to a cottage that had some grass growing on the roof. A woman was trying to get her cow to go up a ladder to the grass, but the poor cow would not go. The young man asked the woman what she was doing.

"Why, look," she said, "look at all that beautiful grass. I'm going to get the cow onto the roof to eat it. She'll be quite safe up there, for I shall tie a rope around her and pass it down the chimney and tie the other end to my waist. Then she can't fall off without my knowing it."

"Oh, you poor silly!" said the young man. "Why don't you cut the grass and throw it down to the cow?"

But the woman thought it easier to get the cow up the ladder than to get the grass down to the cow. So the young man helped her push and coax the cow up to the roof. Then the woman tied a rope around the cow and passed it down the chimney and fastened it to her own waist.

The young man started on his way, but he hadn't gone far when the cow tumbled off the roof and hung by the rope in midair. The weight of the cow pulled the woman up the chimney, where she stuck fast.

Well, thought the young man as he ran back, cut the rope, and helped the woman down, *that's one big silly.*

He started his journey again.

When night fell, he stopped at an inn.

The inn was so full that he was put in a room with another traveler. The other man was a very pleasant fellow, and they got along nicely.

But in the morning, when they were both getting up, the young man was surprised to see the other man hang his trousers on the knobs of the chest of drawers. The man ran across the room and tried to jump into them. He tried over and over again, while the young man wondered what he was doing.

At last the stranger stopped to wipe his face with a handkerchief.

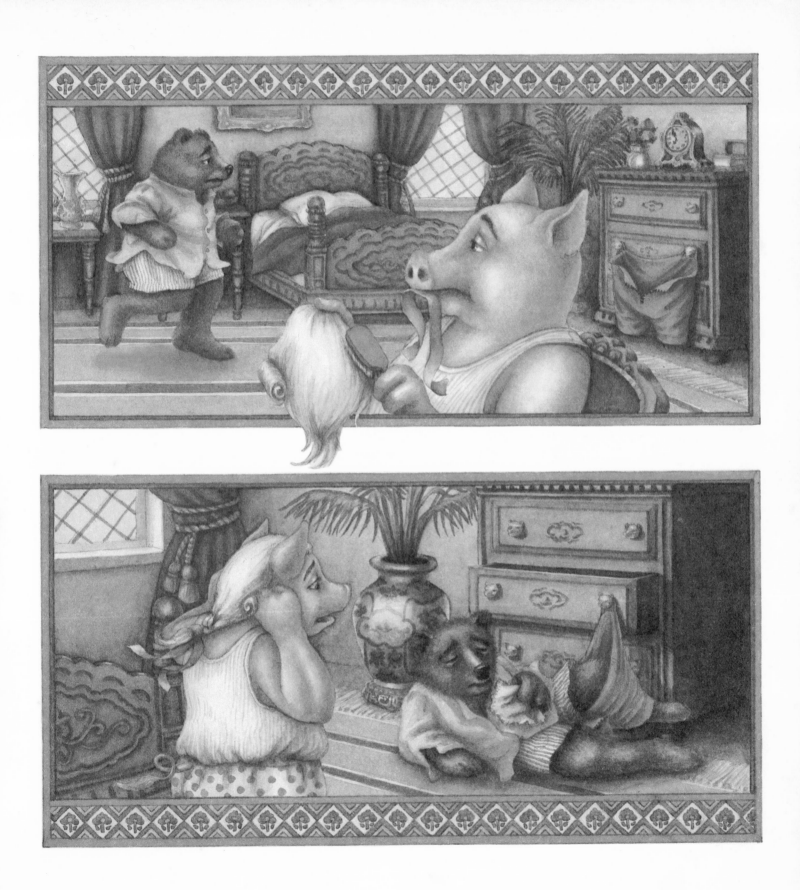

"Oh, dear," he said, "I *do* think trousers are the most awkward kind of clothes. I wonder who could have invented such things. It takes me the best part of an hour to get into mine every morning, and I get so hot! How do you manage yours?"

The young man burst out laughing and showed him how to put trousers on. The stranger was very grateful to the young man and said he hadn't known that getting dressed could be so easy.

So, thought the young man, *that's the second big silly.*

The young man set off on his travels again.

That evening, he came to a village, and outside the village
was a pond, and around the pond was a crowd of people.
They all were reaching into the pond with rakes and brooms
and pitchforks. The young man asked what was the matter.

"Why," they said, "what's the matter? The moon has tumbled into the pond, and we can't fetch it out!"

The young man laughed and told them to look in the sky. "It's only a reflection of the moon in the water," he said.

But the villagers refused to listen to him. With a shout,
they began to chase him, shaking their fists and waving their
pitchforks. The young man ran away as quickly as he could.

Well, he thought, *there are a good many sillies bigger than those three sillies at home.*

So the young man went back home and married the farmer's daughter, and they lived happily forever after.

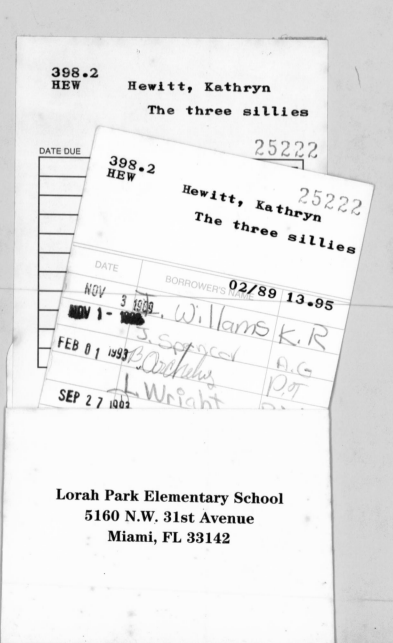

398.2
HEW

Hewitt, Kathryn

The three sillies

25222

398.2
HEW

Hewitt, Kathryn

25222

The three sillies

02/89 13.95

DATE	BORROWER'S NAME	
NOV 3 1989	J. Willams	K. R
NOV 1 - 1992		
FEB 01 1993	J. Spencer	A. G
	B. Archelus	P. T
SEP 27 1993	L. Wright	